S0-BAN-709

THE BASILICA OF THE
Sagrada Familia

ANTONI GAUDÍ'S MOST IMPORTANT CREATION

PHOTOGRAPHS: CARLOS GIORDANO RODRÍGUEZ AND NICOLÁS PALMISANO SOSA

DOSDEARTE EDICIONES

ANTONI GAUDÍ (1852-1926)

Contents

The basilica's origins

Monumental work
Provided with extraordinary dimensions, the Basilica of the Sagrada Familia converted into the city's new reference point.

The nineteenth century was a complicated period for Christianity in Europe, and Barcelona, a city that was undergoing great social and economic change during this period, was a paradigm of these difficulties. The Church, which had wielded great influence throughout the entire history of Spain, saw its authority greatly challenged due to the action of the successive liberal governments that held power in the decades following the French Revolution and the War of Independence. The ecclesiastical confiscations dictated in 1836, whereby the State expropriated lands and assets that the Church had accumulated over the centuries, plunged the institution into a deep economic crisis. Moreover, a section of Spanish society had to undergo a radical change in habits brought about by the Industrial Revolution and by the consequent shift from eminently rural customs to a new urban lifestyle. This process brought with it a spiritual crisis that the Spanish clergy combatted with the fevered missionary activity of numerous ecclesiastics of the time, determined to recuperate the lost faith of millions of citizens. The foundation in 1866 of the Association of Devotees of Saint Joseph was part of this reaction by the Church to recover its spiritual influence on society. The fact that by 1878 the association already had half a million members encouraged its creator, bookseller and philanthropist Josep Maria Bocabella, to take up the construction of an expiatory temple dedicated to the Holy Family, subsidised by worshippers' donations on a plot of land in the Eixample, the new district drawn up in the city after the demolishment of the medieval walls. After several years of preparation, building work started on the 19th of March, 1882.

The temple's evolution with Gaudí

The architect took charge of the construction project of the Sagrada Familia in the year 1883 and was its director for forty-three years, up until his death in 1926. Just a few weeks after taking on the post he had already totally changed the project, not only its aesthetic and structural appearance, but in the magnitude and significance of the work. After introducing subtle but relevant changes in the crypt –started before his arrival– Antoni Gaudí shows off all his creative genius on the apse, the cloister and the Nativity façade, his great architectonic legacy, and leaves his successors a detailed constructive plan that includes solutions full of ingenuity and originality for the naves and the towers that have to top the arrangement.

The architect's milestone
Sagrada Familia demonstrates Gaudí's stylistic evolution, where innovations developed in other commissions were incorporated into the project.

The crypt

The crypt, a word whose Greek origin means hidden, is an underground space commonplace in medieval churches. Its source goes back to the mausoleums that were excavated in rocky zones where martyrs were laid to rest during the early years of Christianity, in order to protect remains from desecration in a period in which the Christian faith was clandestine. Centuries on, when these martyrs were canonized, it became common practice to build a temple over the crypt where the body was kept, so that they could be venerated and their memory properly honoured. From this ancient practice arose the layout typical of crypts in Romanesque and Gothic churches: they are vaulted spaces that are much lower than the temples covering them and they are supported by thick pillars which are capable of withstanding the weight of the building that towers above. Normally located below the church's high altar, crypts often reproduce the profile of the presbytery and lack natural light due to the fact that they are underground. Equipped with this historical and architectonic knowledge, Gaudí assumes the task of the Sagrada Familia and immediately leaves his own particular stamp on the construction of the crypt, started the year before by his predecessor Francesc del Villar. Although he took on the project set on maintaining the former neo-Gothic style, he was capable of converting this space –traditionally dark, enclosed and with low ceilings– into a spacious area that was brighter and better ventilated. These modifications radically changed the arrangement and made it apt for worship where, since 1930, it has been used as Sagrada Familia's parish. It was designated a World Heritage site in the year 2005.

Angels
With their presence felt throughout the crypt, on the stained glass they seem child-like and simply drawn, while on the keystones and corbels they are more realistically portrayed.

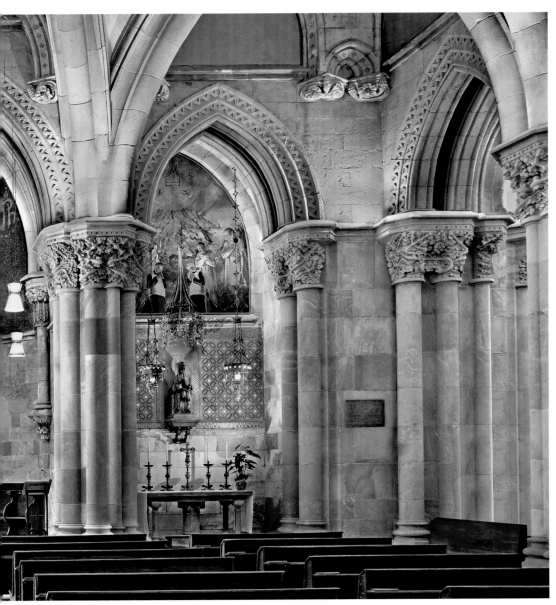

The twelve chapels

The crypt's chapels are organised into two groups. On one side, the apse chapels, dedicated to saints related to the Holy Family and other advocations, are dedicated to Saint Elisabeth and Saint Zachariah –the Virgin's cousins–, the Immaculate Conception, Saint Joseph –the Holy Family's patriarch and patron of the association founded by the temple's developer–, the Sacred Heart of Jesus, Saint Joachim and Saint Anne –the Virgin's parents– and Saint John the Baptist, son of Elisabeth and Zachariah, and Saint John the Evangelist. On the other side, Gaudí arranged, on the opposite wall, the five other chapels, one of which is also the central altar and is presided over by a modernist carving of the Holy Family. The oratories at the far ends are dedicated to Our Lady of Carmel and to the Holy Christ, and hold the remains of Gaudí and Bocabella.

Craftwork

Shackled by the structural plan of his predecessor's decisions, Antoni Gaudí concentrated in particular on decorative and symbolic aspects in order to give the crypt its own identity. Firstly, he substituted the Corinthian endings planned for the capitals with plant motifs, in accordance with his naturalistic conception of architecture. Once the crypt's structure was concluded, he designed the symbolic program of the chapels with the supervision of Bocabella and the aid of numerous artists and craftsmen close to him. That is to say, Gaudí had winged angels sculpted –to be used as column pedestals–, he proposed the mosaic theme that decorates the paving of the central area and designed the sacristy door and the keystones that decorate the vaults, as well as the stained glass windows and the lamps that illuminate the chapels.

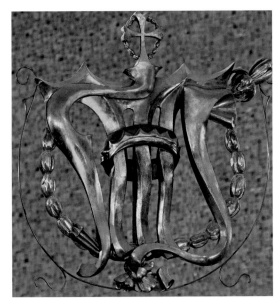

The ambulatory. Of semi-circular shape, the corridor that separates the chapels from the central area of the crypt is covered by eleven Gothic cross vaults.

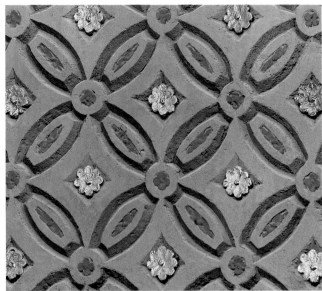

Symbology
Gaudí used quite a large variety of materials for the decoration of the crypt, following a strict symbolic program.

Central vault
The architect designed a ribbed, gothically inspired roof higher than the rest.

The cross vaults

For its underground location and below the tremendous weight of the apse walls, the crypt of the Basilica of the Sagrada Familia stays up thanks to two concentric rows of large pillars of oval section, which form ogival archways and support the weight of a total of 22 Gothic style ribbed cross vaults. Ten of them cover the chapels of the arrangement, another eleven make up the ambulatory and the largest covers the centre of the crypt with a complex radial solution based on twelve ribs that stem from a large keystone decorated with a scene from the Annunciation, work of sculptor Joan Flotats. This central vault goes two metres above the ceilings surrounding it. This difference, meant the architect could put openings high up in the arches, overlooking the basilica's interior to provide more light and ventilation.

Keystone relief of the central vault. Depicting Mary's Annunciation, it was sculpted and polychromed by Joan Flotats.

The apse

The presbytery vault
A forest of columns arranged in a circle converge over the main altar, converting the vault into a large skylight.

The Christian faith of Antoni Gaudí grew in an exponential way during the forty-three years he was at the helm of the building work on the Sagrada Familia, due to a constant feedback between the temple and its creator. Actually, from a very early age he had already professed a fervent devotion to the Virgin Mary, built up throughout his childhood and youth in his native city –Reus–, whose patron saint is the Madonna of Mercy. In fact, the worship of Mary experienced an age of splendour in the second half of the 19th century, in particular dating from 1854, when Pope Pius IX proclaimed the Dogma of the Immaculate Conception. Imbued by this existing devotion to the Virgin in Europe and by his own Marian convictions, Gaudí decided to dedicate the entire arrangement of constructions on the apse's façade –Mary's tower, the apse and the Assumption Chapel– to Jesus' mother and, as a counterpoint, he dedicated the seven interior chapels of the temple's chevet to the Sorrows and Joys of Saint Joseph by express wish of Josep Maria Bocabella, developer of the work. In this way Antoni Gaudí –well read on the history of ecclesiastical architecture and Christian symbolism– provides each one of the façades of the Basilica of the Sagrada Familia with a defined significance, with the apse being chosen to hold the greater number of Marian elements. Precisely for this reason and continuing with this allegorical coherence, the architect decides to locate one of the six cimborios planned for the temple on the apse side: a monumental tower reaching 130 metres high with a sculpture that represents the *Stella Matutina* or the Morning Star, an ancient Marian image that symbolises the dawn and dusk of each day.

The naturalistic vision of Gaudí

Antoni Gaudí was a great observer of nature. He had a deep admiration for all living things and, in particular, plants and trees, which on numerous occasions were a source of inspiration in the aesthetic as well as technical sense. On one occasion he went so far as to say that his master was a tree which was growing near his workshop. Representations from the vegetable kingdom are frequent in his work, like the ears of wheat and floral motifs that top the pinnacles of the apse walls.

The gargoyles

In the Gothic period, gargoyles commonly represented fantastical beings and creatures of demonic character. On the apse of the Sagrada Familia, Gaudí preferred to use more realistic figures and resorted to common animals –traditionally associated with evil– and he positioned them face down, fleeing from the purity that emanates from the Virgin Mary's symbols.

The interior of the apse

Continuing with the symbolic coherence of the basilica, Gaudí dedicated the apsidal chapels to the seven sorrows and joys of Saint Joseph and provided them with separate spaces –of pentagonal structure– facing the ambulatory, in a free interpretation of medieval Gothic cathedrals where height, illumination and sound were three fundamental concepts. In that sense he planned the chapels in such a way to receive light from two areas: on one side from the large, Gothic style windows –designed to be filled with different coloured stained glass– and, on the other, from higher up by means of the lanterns. The third concept, sound, he also decided to introduce it into the apse, by putting over the seven chapels –and throughout the length of the apse's entire perimeter– the continuation of the choir gallery of the nave used for the child choir.

The angels on the corbels

Inspired by the ornamental and symbolic solution used by Antoni Gaudí in the crypt, sculptor Jaume Cases designed stone angels to decorate the columns of the chapels of the apse. Subsequently the two levels of the temple share iconography related to the Book of the Apocalypse of Saint John.

The upper structure of the chevet

Marked by the semi-circular ground plan of the apse, the chevet vertically develops in three stretches, from below to above: the apsidal chapels illuminated by high Gothic windows, decorated with stained glass of abstract theme; the stand with terraces reserved for the choir-stands for the children's choir, culminated by seven lanterns, one over each chapel; and, highest up, the enormous structure of Mary's tower, which tops the arrangement of the apse with a cimborio measuring 130 metres high.

The cloister

A fundamental element in medieval religious architecture, the cloister arose in monasteries as an evolution of the atrium found in Roman dwellings and the first palaeo-Christian basilicas. All the rooms in the monasteries was connected and arranged around this quadrangular, arcaded and generally landscaped courtyard. During the Middle Ages and up to the late nineteenth century, the period in which construction on the Sagrada Familia started, the cloister was a basic element not only for monasteries, but for cathedrals and for the majority of large churches that had to provide rooms for canons or religious orders. It was always put to one side of the church, parallel to the naves, which it was often connected to via a highly ornate portal. However, in the first project of the Sagrada Familia, Francisco del Villar did not foresee the construction of a cloister. In contrast, Antoni Gaudí, whose apprenticeship had been strongly marked by Historicism which extolled the recuperation of medieval styles, took on the work whilst searching for a means to include a cloister in the project. With the crypt already started and located right in the centre of the block meant the traditional layout of an arcaded courtyard would prove to be impossible. Gaudí, however, demonstrated great practicality and proposed a revolutionary solution, never seen before in the history of religious architecture: a cloister that went right around the temple, cutting it off from the hustle and bustle of the surrounding streets and allowing the basilica to be able to enjoy the peaceful and tranquil atmosphere typical of a monastery. With this solution, moreover, the architect recuperated the true significance of the cloister, which is to enclose.

Vault keystone
An angel dancing whilst holding the rosary in its hands is depicted on the keystone on the portal dedicated to the Virgin of the Rosary.

Between the spiritual and earthly

When devising the cloister like a barrier that isolates the basilica, Antoni Gaudí imagined this space as a frontier between the secular –the exterior– and the spiritual –the interior–, a symbolism that he would use years later in the Park Güell project. In this symbolic framework, the Sagrada Familia's cloister represents the earthly world, which the architect conceived as a space for the holding of processions and decorated its doors with roses –symbol of the rosary and, in traditional cloisters, the heavenly–, and with olive branches and palm leaves, which recall Jesus' entrance into Jerusalem. In order to be able to complete the symbolism planned, the architect puts into place, on the cloister's exterior walls, anagrams of the Sagrada Familia or Holy Family, helicoidal columns and elements alluding to nature.

The Holy Family
The anagram is formed by Jesus' cross, Joseph's carpenter's saw and the Virgin Mary's initial.

The Rosary portal. Antoni Gaudí knew he wouldn't be the architect to complete the four portals of the façades and thought he had better leave a finished model behind so those who continued on with his work would have a prototype they could refer to and follow. With this idea he dedicates the only portico that he got to finish to the Rosary Virgin, in which he designed a complex and detailed arch with two archivolts decorated with sculptures of characters from the Old Testament, illuminated zenithally by a conically shaped lantern. On this same line, he arranged the sculptures of the Rosary Virgin and Saints Domingo and Catalina on the portal's tympanum. Despite his efforts to leave his legacy behind, the original sculptures on this portal were destroyed in 1936 with the anticlerical assaults that occurred during the first days of the Civil War.

>>
Roses sculpted out of stone

In honour of the Rosary Virgin, all the constructive elements that make up the portal – such as the walls, the vaults and the arches– are decorated with ros- es carved from stone, one of the most com- monly used symbols to represent the Virgin Mary in general and to the dedication of the Rosary in particular.

>>
Allegorical ornamentation

The walls of the Rosary Portal are heavily adorned with sculpted phrases and details of Marian character, such as crowns and plant decoration.

<<
The Virgin of the Rosary

The central sculpture of the tympanum represents the Marian dedication to which the entire portal is dedicated to, with Mary holding her son in her arms.

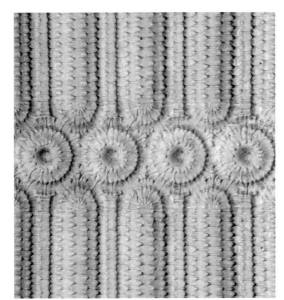

The interior

In Ancient Greece, the agora or main meeting point incorporated a *stoa basiliké*, a large space where justice was carried out, divided into three naves by two rows of columns. This building was used by the Romans for the same purpose and with a similar layout: it was an edifice of rectangular ground plan, with three or five naves –the central one with the highest ceiling– and a raised gallery from which judges presided over trials. From the fourteenth century, with Emperor Constantine's conversion to Christianity, basilicas transformed into places of worship for the new religion, with these columned structures of ancient civic tradition used as models for churches. This progressive Christianisation of basilicas led to a key change in this type of building: the adoption of the cross ground plan, a shape that symbolises the presence of Christ in the temple and which is defined with the addition of a nave –also known as the transept– that transversely crosses the basilica. The passing of the centuries and varying artistic styles did not change this layout, to the point that, in 1883, when taking charge of the management of Sagrada Familia, Gaudí found himself with a project that implied the construction of an interior with a Latin cross ground plan, a scheme in which the transept is found closer to the head of the church. Sensible yet daring at the same time, Antoni Gaudí conserved the layout of the ground plan –which he only retouched in order to increase it to five naves– and ploughed all his creative energy in search of a revolutionary solution for the vertical projection of the temple, marked by an avant-garde structure that dispensed with buttresses thanks to the invention of arborescent columns and hyperbolic vaults.

Catalan vault
Antoni Gaudí reinterpreted the traditional system of the brick vault for the roof of the central nave.

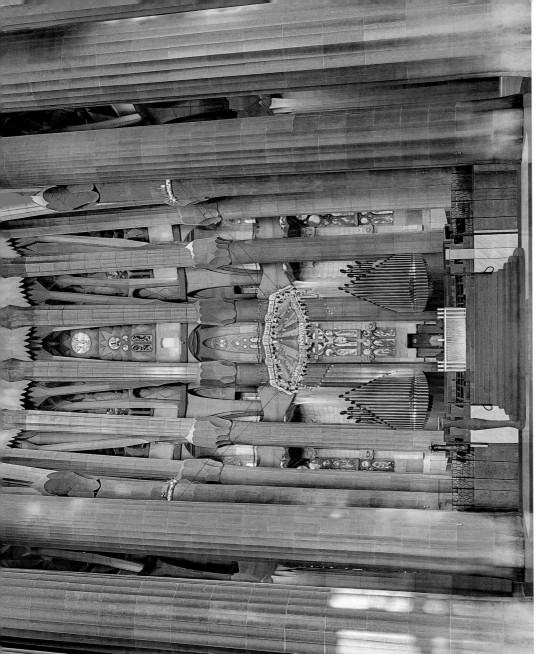

A mystic forest. Gaudí wanted to convert the inside of the Basilica of the Sagrada Familia into a large forest in which the structure of columns, vaults and roofs would work by imitating trees, with the trunk, the branches and, covering the structure, the foliage which the sun light filters through. This innovative solution was designed to create a transcendental atmosphere appropriate for prayer and meditation and to provoke a contrast with the ground plan, in which the architect opted for a traditional structure of five naves, divided up by four rows of columns and crosscut by a transept, and a presbytery where the high altar is found –significantly raised above the level of the rest of the temple–, an ambulatory and seven radial chapels.

Movement around the basilica

In order to be able to guarantee correct, free and natural movement, whether for worshippers or clergy, throughout the different parts of the temple, Gaudí plans a system of winding staircases –two alongside the apse and the transept and two over the Glory's interior façade– and several corridors with the purpose of connecting the different areas of the basilica. To carry out this idea, the architect follows the classical guidelines of medieval cathedrals and creates a series of triforiums of differing height that go around most of the temple's perimeter.

The high altar and the baldachin. As the main nucleus of the basilica, the altar is situated at the point where two of the temple's most important axis converge: on one side, the via humanitatis, which runs from the centre of the Glory façade until midway through the apse's central chapel, and, on the other, the line that goes through the crypt, the altar and Mary's cimborio –the tower that culminates the presbytery and tops the apse–, an axis that perpendicularly crosses the other path. Precisely in conjunction with this last imaginary line, the baldachin that covers the high altar, a structure inspired by the same element planned by Antoni Gaudí for Mallorca Cathedral in 1912. From the baldachin's framework hang Jesus' cross, the vine and wheat –symbol of the Eucharist– and fifty lights, in reference to Saint John Lateran's Basilica, which is Rome's cathedral.

The transept. Antoni Gaudí remained faithful to his convictions and the evocation of medieval architectonic shapes that abounded in the latter half of the nineteenth century. This therefore led to his incorporation of a spacious transept with three naves, whose most important characteristic is their sixty metre height, where the vaults are located that cover the mentioned area and where the basilica's highest tower commences, the cimborio dedicated to Jesus Christ. Supported by twelve columns –four of which are the central pillars dedicated to the Evangelists that support the crossing's vault–, the transept designed by Antoni Gaudí is one of the largest transepts planned in the history of universal ecclesiastical architecture.

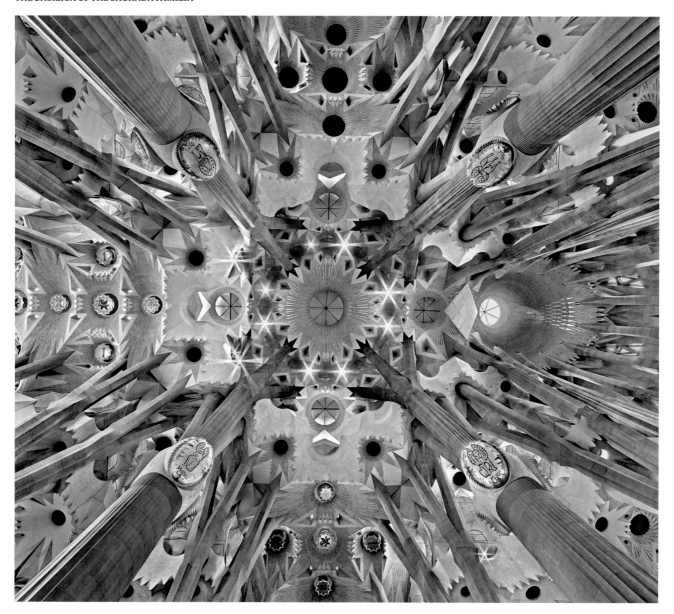

The end of Gaudí's path

Supported by arborescent columns that branch out high up in the basilica, the vaults that cover the naves and the transept represent the culmination of Gaudí's artistic evolution from the modernized neo-Gothic forms of his first project up to the application of the so-called double-ruled surfaces, in this case hyperboloid ones. Light and very easy for light to penetrate through, the interior roof is a sumptuous version of the Catalan bricked vault technique. Widely used in the territory, this highly valued, traditional construction technique is normally devised using solid brickwork, but for the building work on the basilica, it was designed with reinforced concrete on the lateral naves –forming a star-like design– and with ceramic tiles on the central nave, creating a helicoidal layout similar to palm leaves.

The vaults
Gaudí took elements from Gothic art and traditional architecture and applied to them what he had learnt from his observation of nature, devising never seen before structures.

The two interior façades

The north-east south-west orientation of the transept –facing dawn and dusk– is essential in order to illuminate the basilica. Thanks to this layout, as much the openings made in the mentioned walls as the stained glass that covers them carry out a triple function: to light up the temple during the early and late hours of the day, to propose a different and alternative aesthetic solution for each one of the two interior walls with a circular rose window on the east façade and oval one on the west– and to function as a base for a specific symbolic program: the eastern wing is dedicated to Saint Joseph and the western wing, to Jesus' mother, Mary.

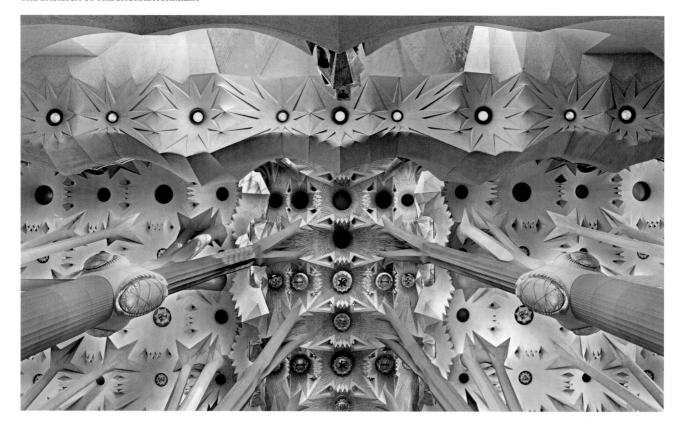

Columns and vaults

The architect drew from nature and got his inspiration from tree trunks when designing the columns, in such a way that the shafts imitate trunks, the capitals are knots, the upper columns branches and the vaults foliage.

Nature as a model

Gaudí investigated for years until he managed to come up with a column that avoided the use of buttresses on walls. Loyal to the teachings of nature, two years before his death, in the year 1924, he was sufficiently inspired to find a definitive solution: the arborescent column. The architect wanted the pillars supporting the temple to combine the strength and beauty of the largest trees. For this reason he fled from the rigid verticality of classical architectonic references and designed columns that tilted in relation to the height they reached in order that they could withstand the loads originating from the roof. The secret lay in turning the column's shaft in two directions –as happens with trees– in order to achieve a better resistance and by branching out the upper section into small columns in order that the nave vaults are adequately supported.

<<
Rose window
Abstract forms abound in Joan Vila-Grau's stained glass work on the Sagrada Familia, an artist that combines a reticle of lead based on straight lines with curved shapes that mark the composition and lend it dynamism. Along with this abstraction, Vila-Grau skilfully selects a wide range of colours and tones for each window, avoiding the mix of cold and warm tones that characterize medieval stained glass windows and he manages to create an almost supernatural atmosphere thanks to the warmth of the light and the reflection of the drawings on the temple's walls.

>>
The custodias
Gaudí designed 24 custodias –Christian liturgical objects used to place the blessed sacrament– to put over the choirstands.

Saint Mark symbol

Saint John symbol

Saint Luke symbol

Saint Matthew symbol

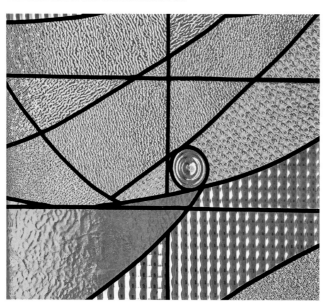

A temple invaded by light

The sturdiness of the load-bearing structure which Gaudí devised after decades of study meant that large zenithal claraboyas of hyperboloid form could be included in the vaults that, along with the enormous hollows made in the walls, illuminate the interior in a harmonious and uniform manner. The diffusers that the architect planned to cover these large openings in the temple's roof allow natural light to filter through which achieves an atmosphere ideal for retreat and prayer in the enormous space occupied by the naves. In the same way, the ogival windows and rose windows of neo-Gothic genre that go round the temple were planned by Gaudí in order to hold a new type of stained glass, with a system created by the architect that consists of superimposing three panes of primary colours, resulting in a combination of new tones.

Stained glass work
One of Gaudí's main concerns at the moment of lightening the walls and the vaults of the temple was to facilitate the entrance of light –the main symbol of Jesus Christ– into the basilica by means of numerous openings.

The Nativity façade

Jesus the carpenter
Llorenç Matamala sculpted the scene of the Son of God helping his father in his workshop.

"It just isn't possible for one sole generation to erect the entire temple. Let's therefore leave behind a vigorous display of our passage, in order that future generations are encouraged to do the same". With these words Gaudí conveyed a combination of modesty, pragmatism and a command of the history of art, by foreseeing that the construction of the Sagrada Familia would follow the same pace as the great medieval cathedrals and which he would only get to see just started. This vigorous display that the architect referred to was the Nativity façade, whose construction work lasted 41 years and was completed in 1936 –ten years after the accidental death of the artist– with the culmination of the pinnacles of the three portals that make it up. This façade is the only part of the basilica that Gaudí totally designed and which he got to see almost finished, with the result that it has converted into the most Gaudían universal paradigm of the Sagrada Familia, achieving the goal set by the architect when planning it: to serve as an example in order that those who continue on with his work may observe the sculptural and decorative terminations that he envisaged for the totality of the work. If this has been made possible, it is largely thanks to the donations of well-to-do Barcelonan families which allowed Gaudí to realize the complex decorative program that he had devised for the façade. Another influencing factor was the determination of the work's administrator, who pressured the architect to rapidly invest the money in models and material, artists and the workmen necessary to raise the façade, before the bishop and the Barcelonan diocese could spread donations out amongst other projects, common practice at the time.

Three porticos below four towers. Although Gaudí considered the Gothic as an "imperfect" genre, with the Nativity façade he followed a scheme typical of this style and structured it around three porticos -a central one and two lateral ones- accompanied by four bell towers on the eastern side and lodged in the hollows of these towers' bases. The architect dedicated them to the three members of the Holy Family, each linked to a theological virtue: the portico on the left represents Hope, a virtue associated to Saint Joseph; the central one, dedicated to Jesus, represents Charity, which is topped by a naturalist pinnacle –The Tree of Life– which competes in height with the towers, and the portico on the right represents Faith, personified by the Virgin Mary.

Between heaven and earth

Despite being just a side entrance to the basilica, Antoni Gaudí positioned two monumental columns on the Nativity façade –in the style of the main entrances of great temples– and arranged them separating the three porticos that make it up. Attached to the wall the columns possess a very tall trunk with spiralling indents and in the centre have much wider carved stone decorated with plant motifs that incorporate the names of the figures to whom they are dedicated: Saint Joseph is on the left and the Virgin Mary is on the right. Both columns represent the connection between the secular world and the heavenly world and are finished off by naturalist capitals that emulate palm leaves from which grow numerous bunches of dates and which provide support for the trumpeting angels that culminate the arrangement.

The Hope portico. Although it does not reach the height of the central portal, the Hope portico combines some marked vertical proportions, which are ideal for displaying the mountainous surroundings that are inspired by the massif of Montserrat (Barcelona), and a context of flora and aquatic fauna that reminds of the banks of the River Nile, in consonance with one of the main scenes represented: the Holy Family fleeing to Egypt after an angel appears in Joseph's dreams, warning him of the Slaughter of the Innocents. This last biblical fact, also shown on the portico, makes up the goriest sculptural group on the whole façade.

<<
The Flight to Egypt
Sculpted by Llorenç Matamala and Carles Mani, the sculptural group shows an angel guiding the Holy Family that is escaping to Egypt to avoid the death of Jesus.

>>
The Slaughter of the Innocents
Following the orders of King Herod, a legionnaire with indifferent expression sets about killing a newborn while he ignores the pleas of its mother, in a dramatic scene that contrasts with the general joy that is transmitted by the Nativity façade.

Betrothal of the Virgin Mary and Saint Joseph

Saint Joseph's pinnacle

To go under the crags that culminate the Hope portico, Gaudí had Llorenç Matamala's studio create the figure of Saint Joseph navigating a boat, a vessel that symbolises the passage of the Catholic Church, whose helmsman is the patriarch of the Holy Family and father of the Church. The cave the boat crosses and the darkness surrounding it represents the difficulties that Saint Joseph will face on his way, while the underground waters that the boat sails through stand for spiritual purity and regeneration. The fact that this imaginary river flows below a sculptural piece inspired by the rounded shapes of the Massif of Montserrat is interpreted as a homage to the Patron Saint of Catalonia, whose Romanesque carving was found by some young shepherds inside a cave in the above mentioned mountainous zone, near Barcelona.

Saint Joseph
The likeness to Gaudí is an apparent homage by the workers of the temple following his death.

The Charity portico

Dedicated to Jesus and to the third theological virtue –the other two are Faith and Hope–, the Charity portico takes up the central and largest space of the Nativity façade. Practically indiscernible due to the sculptural and ornamental detail that Gaudí devised for the main entrance to the temple from the eastern side, the walls of this portico create a concave space that generates a large scale cave that depicts the stable scene where the Messiah was born. Moreover, the sculptural groups on this portico display the different protagonists that are associated with the birth of Jesus with up to thirty-three human figures depicted in stone, as well as a large number of plants and domestic animals –particularly birds– which contribute with their aura of innocence to the celebration of the arrival of the Messiah.

Jesus' column

Gaudí had the sculptural arrangement of the Nativity put into place –symbolic centre of the façade of the same name– over the column of the mullion of the Charity portico that precedes the entrance to the basilica interior. However, it wasn't until the 19th of March 1958 –Saint Joseph's Day– when the definitive arrangement was installed, work of sculptor Jaume Busquets, modernist artist Joan Llimona's apprentice and, from an early age, Gaudí's too. The composition created by Busquets, with the ox and mule surrounding the Nativity scene, focuses the spectator's attention on the figure of the Child –at the same time protected and exhibited by the Virgin– and carries out the function of focal point amongst surrounding sculptures.

The signs of the zodiac. The vault over the Annunciation depicts the constellations just as they were the night that Jesus was born.

The Annunciation. This work by Jaume Busquets shows the moment that the archangel Gabriel tells Mary that she has been chosen to bring the Son of God into the world.

The angel musicians
Surrounding the Nativity's central scene, slightly higher up, a chorus of young angels celebrate the good news accompanied by six musicians that play instruments used in religious and popular music.

Nature on the portico

For the decoration of the Charity portico Antoni Gaudí devised a clearly defined program that was based on impact and symbolism. In order to carry off his scheme he decides to smother the walls with biblical representations associated with Jesus' life and above all Christmas traditions, a setting that provides warmth and popularity to the decorative program. In this sense, each representation responds to a defined symbolism: the birds, due to their ability to fly, are messengers between Heaven and Earth, in contrast to the serpent, who embodies all that is terrestrial. The abundance of flowers, in contrast, represents the blossoming of springtime, associated with the birth of a new cycle, while the cypress tree that dominates the portico symbolises the passing of time and the doves allude to the presence of the Holy Spirit.

The Crowning of the Virgin Mary. Work of Joan Matamala, it depicts the moment that the Virgin is crowned as recompense for her selfless love of God.

The Tree of Life

Gaudí reserved the top part of the portico for the representation of the Tree of Life, symbolic compendium of the three porticos that make up the Nativity façade and allegory of the triumph of Jesus' legacy. The tree, a cypress, symbolises eternity due to the evergreen of its leaves and its hard-wearing wood. Its green hue stands out from the stone context of the façade, hinting at the effect that would have been created by the application of the idea Gaudí had deliberated over for many years: to polychrome all the sculptural elements of the basilica. The architect had the cypress crowned with the sign of the Holy Trinity and proposed a total of twenty-one white alabaster doves fluttering around the tree; at its base is a pelican, a Eucharist symbol that feeds its offspring and which is situated between two six-runged ladders that represent the aspiration to reach eternal life.

The Visitation

Jesus the carpenter

The Faith portico. In homage to the Virgin, Gaudí had sculptural groups of the Immaculate Conception and the Visitation to Saint Elizabeth sculpted, paradigms of the faith with which Mary assumed the divine plans, main symbolic motif on the portico. Other sculptural groups describe scenes related to the Son of God: the presentation of Jesus in the Temple of Jerusalem –a ritual of initiation that Hebrew parents used to carry out with their newly born children– and the preaching of Jesus in the same temple, provoking the admiration of his own parents, who observe him from lower down. However, the figure that produces a closeness for its size, simplicity and naturalness is the daily representation of Jesus working as a carpenter.

The Virgin Mary

Saint John the Baptist, Jesus Christ's cousin

Jesus in Simeon's arms. The group of the Presentation of Jesus in the Temple depicts the Messiah in Priest Simeon's arms.

Anagram of Saint Joseph. Situated below the Blessed Virgin, the symbol of Jesus' father includes grapes, lilies and shavings.

The Passion façade

Soldiers
The sculptor Josep Maria Subirachs was inspired by La Pedrera's chimneys when creating the soldiers on the Passion façade.

When devising the general project of the basilica, Antoni Gaudí decided to dedicate the temple's three façades to the most transcendental moments of Jesus' life: the Nativity, the Passion and the Glory. During this period, in the early 1890's, Gaudí was already planning to provide the Passion façade with a rather sinister air and believed that if he started off his iconographic project with this portal it might prove to be counterproductive, which subsequently led him to believe that the Nativity, the festive façade, ought to be constructed first. Two decades on, in the year 1911, with the Nativity façade still unfinished, the architect fell ill with Maltese fever and moved to the Pyrenean town of Puigcerdà whose cleaner air would help him recuperate quicker than if he were in industrialised Barcelona. During his forced convalescence, Gaudí came close to death –he even drew up a will–, and this inspired him to finish off the façade that was to relate the final days of Jesus' life; he did it immersed in this spirit of anguish and later acknowledged that he wanted this façade to unnerve its viewers. The result were the sketches that served as inspiration in order that construction work on the temple was taken up again in 1954 on this façade, despite Gaudí having only outlined its decorative details, leaving future generations with the task of interpreting the sculptural programme. This labour was taken on, in the year 1986 –once the structure of the portico and the four bell towers were completed–, by sculptor Josep Maria Subirachs, who took great pains to capture all the distress and sorrow that Gaudí had envisaged for this façade which is oriented, loaded with symbolism, towards the sunset.

The representation of pain

Gaudí devised the Passion façade to be stark and restrained in order to convey the severity of the sacrifice of Jesus. On the nude lines of the walls twelve sculptural groups stand out whose purpose is to explain the hours that passed between the Last Supper and the Resurrection of Jesus Christ, in a sequence that freely interprets the Stations of the Cross –the Pathway to Calvary– that is chronologically developed creating a large 'S' on the façade. In front of the wall, six tilted columns increase the sensation of nudity. Their grooves reach out without ornamental interruptions conjuring up enormous sequoias that support a roof over which Gaudí planned a pediment that was composed of 18 bonelike pillars.

Jesus' last night

In the chronological account of the Passion of Jesus represented on the portico, the first sculptural group is the one situated on the lower left-hand side, which reproduces the Last Supper. On it, the gaunt and abstract faces of the Messiah and his apostles, so characteristic of Subirach's style, convey the affliction and grief of the moment in which Jesus, with his back turned, in the centre of the composition, explains to his disciples the facts about to take place, whilst Judas, at one side, secretly clasps the betrayal money. To the right, between the Gethsemane and the Gospel doorways, the narrative thread of The Passion continues with the scene in which Peter faces the soldiers and the moment in which Judas kisses Jesus to indicate whom they have to arrest, a sculpture in which the artist manages to get over the tense atmosphere.

The Last Supper
Subirachs opted for an unprecedented composition in the history of art when depicting this scene, with Jesus' back to the viewer and the disciples in a semi-circle.

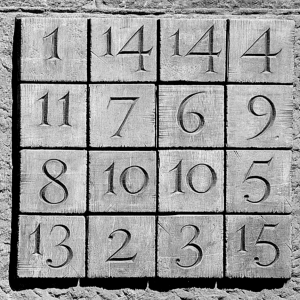

Peter's denial. The three women symbolise the three times that Peter denied knowing Jesus. The apostle is upset by his own cowardice.

Ecce Homo. After being flogged, Jesus is presented before the people wearing a crown of thorns. Pilate is sitting down overwhelmed by the decision he has to make.

The column of Jesus' solitude
Five metres high, this group is placed, symbolically, between Judas, Jesus' betrayer, and Peter, who on three occasions denied all knowledge of him.

The Flagellation

Subirachs gave a special relevance to one of the stations of the Way of the Cross – the Flagellation of Christ– providing it with a sculptural group separate from the wall and in a prime position, opposite the door's mullion, at the same height of all those who enter and leave the temple. Carved in travertine, the flagellation shows Jesus alone and dejected, tied to a column, after being tortured by the legionnaires. The sculptor put this group in the centre of the façade, forming a narrative unit with the sculptures of the Crucifixion –high up on the portico– and the Ascension, on the bridge joining the two central towers. The three steps over which the column rises symbolise the days that passed between the Crucifixion and the Resurrection.

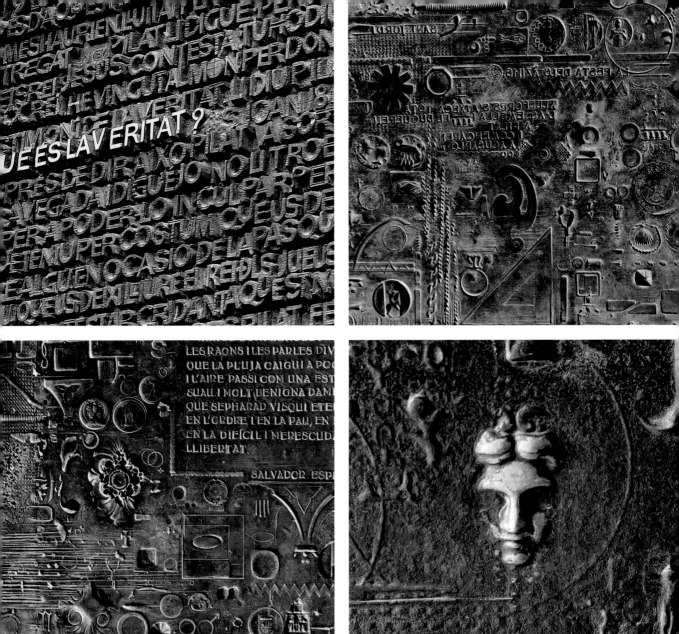

The Gospel doors
Gaudí devised three doors for the façade: the Gospel one, in the centre; the Gethsemane one, to the left, and the Coronation of Thorns, to the right. The central entrance is situated behind the Flagellation and it is divided into two doors measuring almost six metres high that explain, with raised lettering, what the sculptures of the façade express in stone: the Gospel texts relating to Jesus' last two days. The Gethsemane Door illustrates by means of embossed letters Jesus' prayers in the garden and the weakness of the disciples that accompanied him, while the Coronation of Thorns door holds a relief on the upper section that represents the humiliation that the soldiers inflicted on Jesus after torturing him and, in the central section, the scenes of the Presentation of the Messiah before Herod and Pontius Pilate.

Simon of Cyrene and Three Marys. This group is a representation of Jesus' third fall.

Longinus. The soldier pierces the façade with his lance. >>

To the crucifixion
Situated over the Gospel door, the central sculptural arrangement of the intermediate level symbolises Veronica's veil, a scene that narrates the second fall of Jesus on the Way of the Cross and the meeting with the women of Jerusalem, one of whom –Veronica– wipes blood off Jesus' face with a cloth or veil and is left with an image of the Messiah imprinted on it. Carved in bas-relief, Jesus' face always seems to be looking at the observer, no matter where the latter's location; the figure of Veronica, in contrast, lacks features, in order to symbolically reinforce the face of the Messiah stamped on the cloth. The soldiers that accompany the scene, inspired by the chimneys of La Pedrera, are a homage by Subirachs to Gaudí.

The Death of Jesus

In the Crucifixion group, Jesus is tied to a cross composed of two iron beams, one of whose profiles are painted in red to highlight the 'I' of INRI, initials from the Latin inscription "Jesus of Nazareth, King of the Jews" that the Romans put over the cross. At the feet of the Messiah, is Mary Magdalene, knelt, Mary of Cleophas and the Virgin, with her face covered and consoled by Saint John. At the base of the cross, a skull symbolises death and the name of the place where Christ was crucified –Gólgota means 'cranium' in Aramaic–, while the open tomb presages the Resurrection. To the left of the group, Subirachs represented the scene of the soldiers that share out the apparel of the condemned man, and to the right, the burial of Christ, composed as an immense Pieta, in which Mary, Joseph of Arimathea and Nicodemus deposit Jesus' body in the tomb.

The Ascension of Christ. The Passion façade is crowned by a bronze sculpture situated 60 metres high that represents Jesus Christ when he rose to Heaven. Located on the bridge that joins the towers dedicated to Bartholomew and Thomas, the figure –which measures five metres high and weighs two tonnes– completes the iconographic programme of the façade, referring to Christ's union with God after leaving behind the suffering related to the episodes of the Passion and his death. Immersed in this redemptive idea, the Messiah opens his arms to bid farewell to his disciples and to all the worshippers that await his return, transmitting a message of hope that contrasts with the dramatic tone of the sculptural groups situated on the lower levels.

The Glory façade

With the aim of leaving something behind for his successors to refer to, in 1916 –ten years before his death– the architect carried out an indepth study of the constructive structure and the symbolic plan that the Glory façade should have. In order to support his decisions, as was his custom, he had a model made up to demonstrate its total volume and on which the ideas he had devised for the basilica's largest façade could be seen applied. However, this model –the best guide that architects posterior to Gaudí could have counted on in order to carry out the façade– was destroyed in the year 1936, by the fire in the temple's workshop during the uprising at the start of the Civil War. Nowadays, this study model can be found partially reconstructed, but the most significant legacy for the construction of this façade have been the photographs and accounts left behind by the selfsame architect and his collaborators. Nonetheless, one of the aspects where there is much more documentation is that which is related to the urban development project of the temple's surroundings and, above all, what corresponds to the Glory façade that Antoni Gaudí left for implementation. The project conceives a large platform followed by a vast flight of steps that gets over the more than five metre drop between the naves –that of the main floor– and the road. On this platform the architect puts two large monuments –dedicated to water and fire– and underneath devises a tunnel which the traffic will pass through on Mallorca Street. However, one of the most important aspects is the landscaped esplanade that runs in front of the temple with the objective of obtaining a better view of the Glory façade and the entire arrangement.

The Eucharist door
The central portal providing access to the temple reproduces all of the Lord's Prayer.

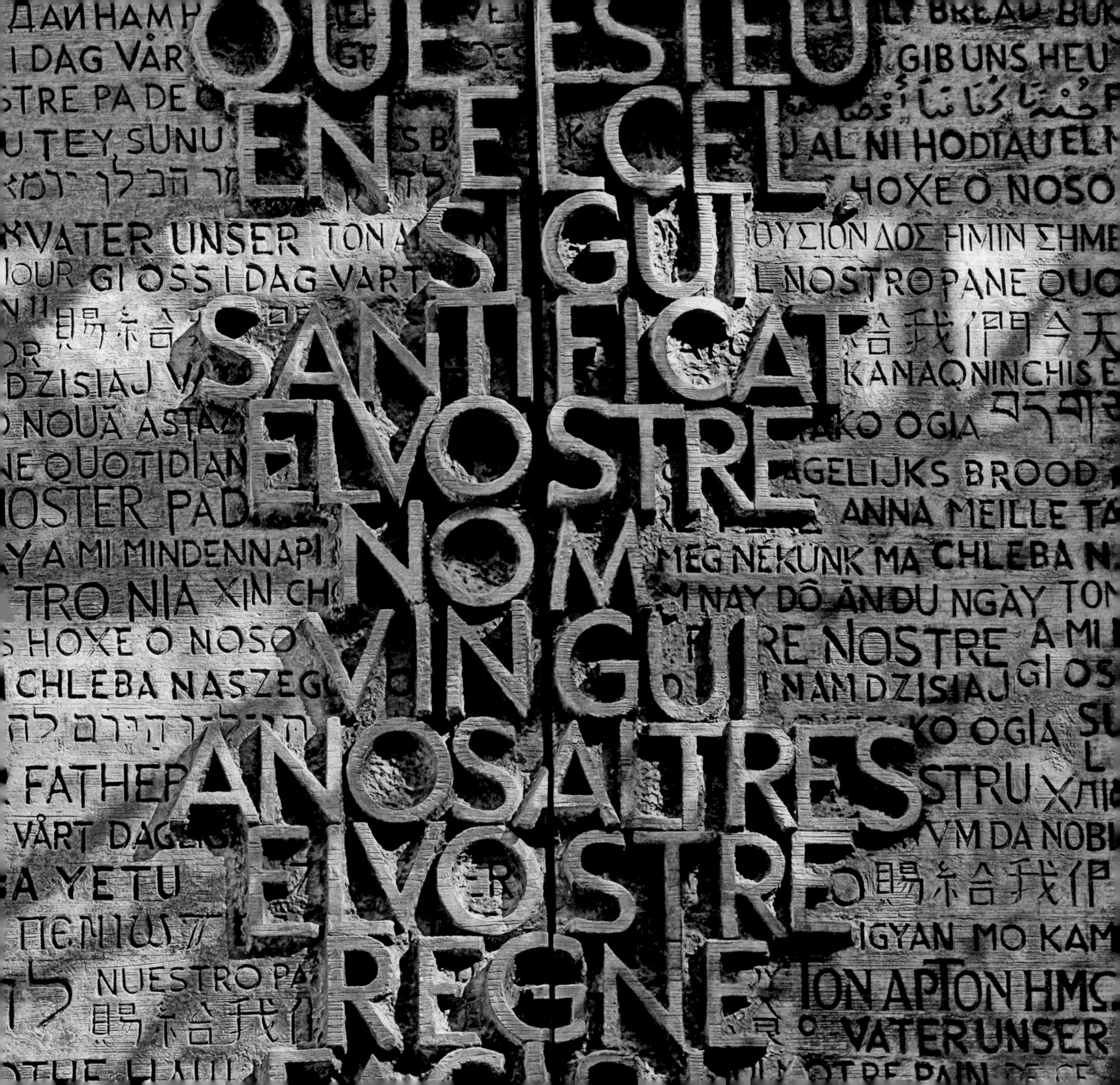
QUE ESTEU
EN EL CEL
SIGUI
SANTIFICAT
EL VOSTRE
NOM
VINGUI
A NOSALTRES
EL VOSTRE
REGNE

RE
DO
LA FE

L'ESPERIT

ELS BISBES, ELS PREVERES ALS DIAQUES

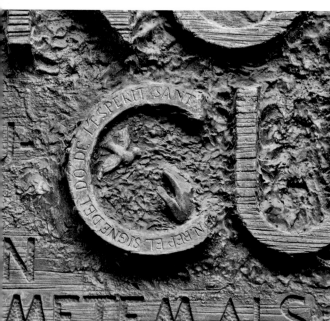

EN REP EL SIGNE DEL DO DE L'ESPERIT SANT

N

METEMAIS

AIGUA

Fifteen columns and seven doors

The portico that precedes access to the temple forms a wide atrium covered by hyperboloid vaults and supported by two rows of columns: seven ones tilting outwardly in the foreground with eight vertical ones in the background. Each one of the exterior columns has the name engraved of one of the seven gifts from the Holy Spirit, while on the bases appear the seven capital sins, and on the capitals, the opposing virtues. Half hidden amongst the interior columns are the seven doors accessing the naves, dedicated to the sacraments of the church and to a petition of The Lord's Prayer. Each one of the portico's doors connects with one of the naves of the temple, except for the main central one, which is divided into three openings.

>>

Gaudí's model

It reproduces in plaster the shapes devised by the architect for the Glory façade.

125

The towers

In any period or civilization religious constructions have stood apart for their monumentality and dimensions, and in particular for their height, a quality that bestows prestige and dignity on a building and is, in itself, a mystic symbol, given that it represents the union between heaven and earth. In the Middle Ages, revolutionary Gothic architects managed to build much higher buildings than their predecessors thanks, principally, to the invention of the ogival arch and the cross vault, which managed to lighten the walls and roofs of the temples and, in consequence, meant that cathedrals could reach heights that had been unimaginable until that time. Centuries later, imbued by the same spirit that fired these medieval architects, Antoni Gaudí wanted to convert the Basilica of the Sagrada Familia into the highest construction in Barcelona. With this objective he designed Jesus' tower –the culmination of the temple– to be 172.5 metres high, a measurement that would make it the tallest religious building in the world, but would leave it just a few metres below Montjuïc, the highest hill in the municipality of Barcelona in the late nineteenth century, when building work on the basilica commenced. With this decision, Gaudí showed a great desire to construct a building that would urbanistically mark the city while at the same time venerate and respect God's work –Montjuïc–, which in his opinion Man should never try to exceed. Finally, out of the eighteen towers of the arrangement –the six cimborios dedicated to Jesus, Mary and the Evangelists and the twelve bell towers representing the Apostles– he only got to see one complete: Barnabus' bell tower, finished in 1925, a few months prior to his death.

Shapes and colours
The endings of the towers stand out for their lively polychrome in contrast to the natural grey stone of the rest of the bell tower.

From Earth to Heaven

Provided with an innovative parabolic design, the bell towers created by Gaudí start off with a squared base and around a quarter of the way up undergo a rapid transition transforming into a circular layout that culminates in their characteristic spire-like shape, result of the application of doubly ruled surfaces, a common resource used by the architect in order that he could imitate structures that he observed in nature. The artist proposed this change of ground plan in order to symbolise by means of the towers the path of the tangible or earthly –represented by the square base– to the celestial, a state that materializes in the formal perfection of the circle. Likewise, Gaudí made the most of this structural transformation in order to support on one of the resulting edges the apostle sculpture to whom each bell tower is dedicated.

<<
The Apostles on the Passion façade

The basilica's bell towers on the western façade are dedicated to the Apostles Philip, Thomas, James the Lesser and Bartholomew. As part of the symbolic program on the Passion façade, the sculptures on this side were undertaken by the artist Josep Maria Subirachs and were put into place on the towers between the months of February and October of the year 2000.

\>>
The Apostles on the Nativity façade

The first towers that were completed were those on the eastern façade, dedicated to the Apostles Matthias, Simon, Barnabus and Judas Thaddaeus. The sculptures, work of Llorenç Matamala following the design of Antoni Gaudí, are situated on the point on which the towers adopt the circular section and carry, on both sides and vertically, the name of the saint in Latin.

Cimborios and bell towers. Gaudí devised the elevations of the eighteen towers of the Sagrada Familia in order that they grew in height according to the symbolic hierarchy of whom they represented and in accordance with their position in relation to the centre of the temple's ground plan: Jesus' cimborio culminates the ensemble at 172.5 metres high and is set over the crossing. The four Evangelist cimborios reach 135 metres and rise up flanking the largest cimborio, as well as the Virgin Mary one, which rises 130 metres over the apse. Finally, the twelve bell towers, dedicated to the apostles, rise, in groups of four, on the periphery of the building, over the three porticos providing access, and measure from 98 to 120 metres. In order to get the most out of the visual and symbolic aspect, all the towers culminate in spires clad in glazed ceramic work from the Island of Murano (Italy).

The endings of the bell towers. Gaudí envisaged complex solutions for the terminations of the twelve Apostles' towers. The first consisted of a look-out tower of hexagonal base and pyramidal shape with rings. The second, which was what was finally carried out, tops each bell tower with a 25 metre high pinnacle adorned with polychrome Venetian ceramic work. The architect made the most of the tiles' glossy reflection to highlight, using the technique he invented –trencadis or broken tile cladding–, the symbology assigned to each bell tower: the initial of the Apostle to whom it is dedicated and the elements that distinguish the bishops –continuers of the evangelical work of Jesus' disciples– represented in a schematic way.

The decoration of the towers

As well as the trencadís cladding of Venetian glazed mosaic work employed on the pinnacles of the bell towers, Gaudí devised numerous decorative elements for the towers of the Basilica of the Sagrada Familia, such as the prayers and inscriptions dedicated to the Holy Trinity and carved in the same natural stone employed on the construction of the walls –visible from far away– or attached small size pieces – only perceptible from the balconies of the towers– which provide variety and originality to the arrangement.

The schoolrooms

Access to the schoolrooms
When designing the schoolrooms, Gaudí looked for the utmost simplicity, using basic brick as the main material whilst devising a structure whose curved forms gave a feeling of solidness to the arrangement.

In order to satisfy every necessity related to the construction of such a formidable project such as the Sagrada Familia, Gaudí had to design provisional buildings for the use of workers and their children. One of these functional buildings was the workshop, a construction that encompassed warehouses, studios for artists and craftsmen –where they carried out their works, their sculptures and models– and the architect's own study –where the architect kept the building plans of the temple–. Nonetheless, out of all the annex buildings –the chaplain's residence was another example– those that have undoubtedly aroused the greatest architectonic interest –for their avant-garde structure and aesthetic originality– have been the schoolrooms. The idea of founding a school linked to the Sagrada Familia was thanks to Father Gil Parés i Vilasau, the first chaplain to be custodian of the crypt, who in 1908 proposed that Gaudí construct an inexpensive building that would be used as an education centre for the children of the workers of the temple and for children from modest backgrounds who resided in the neighbourhood. Parés was a keen follower of the educational method of active pedagogy, a very progressive system devised by the Italian Maria Montessori and characterised for its respect for the student as a person, in a period in which corporal punishment was used frequently in the learning process. In order to carry out this project –probably paid for by the architect–, Gaudí had to use all his ingenuity designing a brick building that, despite its structural simplicity and the humbleness of the materials employed, can be included as one of the most representative works of his professional career.

Simple and functional works

With just one floor measuring 24 metres long by 12 metres wide, the building is narrow, with rounded corners, with two partition walls that provide three classrooms and two lavatories at either end. The walls, render-free, are made up of two layers of brick cemented with fast-setting mortar. The constructive technique transgresses traditional methods: the bricks are laid on their larger side –as interior partitions in houses are usually laid– and vertically positioned –in order to make the façade curve more easily–. For the roof, three iron pillars support a master beam of the same material, which runs through the axis of the building and acts as a support to a series of smaller wooden beams, forming a warped roof, light and resistent at the same time.

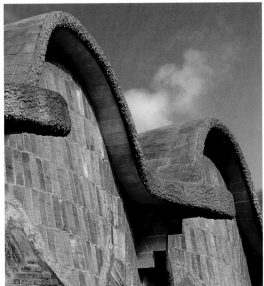

THE BASILICA OF THE SAGRADA FAMILIA

CONCEPT AND MANAGEMENT OF THE PROJECT: CARLOS GIORDANO AND NICOLÁS PALMISANO
COORDINATION: FERNANDO GARCÍA · CONTENTS: DANIEL R. CARUNCHO
PHOTOGRAPHIC RETOUCHING: JAVIER ORDUÑA

PUBLISHED BY
© DOS DE ARTE EDICIONES, S.L., BARCELONA, 2014

TEXTS
MANAGEMENT AND COORDINATION: DOS DE ARTE EDICIONES, S.L.
WRITERS: RICARD REGÀS, DANIEL R. CARUNCHO, CARLOS GIORDANO AND NICOLÁS PALMISANO
TRANSLATION: CERYS GIORDANO JONES
© DOS DE ARTE EDICIONES, S.L., BARCELONA, 2014

ARCHITECTONIC WORK
© JUNTA CONSTRUCTORA DEL TEMPLE EXPIATORI DE LA SAGRADA FAMILIA

PHOTOGRAPHS
AUTHORS: CARLOS GIORDANO AND NICOLÁS PALMISANO
© DOS DE ARTE EDICIONES, S.L., BARCELONA, 2014

WITH THE FOLLOWING EXCEPTIONS:
• PAGES 23, 26-27, 28, 29, 41-63, 123, 124
© JUNTA CONSTRUCTORA DEL TEMPLE EXPIATORI DE LA SAGRADA FAMÍLIA

ARCHIVE PHOTOGRAPHS
• PAGE 3. © ACHILLES (DREAMSTIME.COM)
• PAGE 7. AUTHOR OF THE COLOURING: DANA KELLER. BASED ON AN IMAGE FROM THE PHOTOGRAPHY ARCHIVE
OF THE CENTRE EXCURSIONISTA DE CATALUNYA. © DOS DE ARTE EDICIONES, S.L., BARCELONA, 2014
• PAGE 8. AUTHOR: JOSEP MARIA CO DE TRIOLA . © ARXIU FOTOGRÀFIC CENTRE EXCURSIONISTA DE CATALUNYA
• PAGE 9. AUTHOR: UNKNOWN. ROISIN COLLECTION. © INSTITUT D'ESTUDIS FOTOGRÀFICS DE CATALUNYA
• PAGE 125. © JUNTA CONSTRUCTORA DEL TEMPLE EXPIATORI DE LA SAGRADA FAMÍLIA

FIRST EDITION 2014

ISBN: 978-84-15818-72-4 / DEPÓSITO LEGAL: B 17002-2014 / PRINTED IN SPAIN

ACKNOWLEDGEMENTS
DOS DE ARTE EDICIONES THANKS THE JUNTA CONSTRUCTORA DEL TEMPLE EXPIATORI DE LA SAGRADA FAMÍLIA
FOR ITS COLLABORATION IN THE REALIZATION OF THIS BOOK..

VISIT OUR WEBSITE:
WWW.DOSDEARTE.COM
CONTACT:
PEDIDOS@DOSDEARTE.COM

NO PART OF THIS BOOK MAY BE REPRODUCED, DISTRIBUTED, TRANSFORMED OR PUBLICLY USED
WHETHER TOTALLY OR PARTIALLY, WITHOUT THE PRIOR WRITTEN CONSENT OF THE CORRESPOND-
ING COPYRIGHT OWNERS. THE EDITOR IS AT THE DISPOSITION OF THE OWNERS OF THE RIGHTS OF
POSSIBLE UNIDENTIFIED ICONOGRAPHIC SOURCES.